A long time ago, as a little girl,
I dreamed of traveling all over the world,
And often I'd ask about the past
Driving everyone crazy fast!
Amused by this my parents thought,
Why not call me "History" for short?

Since then I've traveled by land, sea, and air ...

So read this book and I'll take you somewhere!

3

Little Miss HISTORY Travels to
TOMBSTONE ARIZONA

© 2020 Barbara Ann Mojica. All Rights Reserved.

Published in The UNITED STATES of AMERICA
eugenus® STUDIOS, LLC
P.O. BOX 213
Valatie, NY 12184
E-Mail: Barbara@LittleMissHISTORY.com
WebSite: www.LittleMissHISTORY.com

ISBN-13: 978-0-9989154-9-4
Library of Congress Control Number:2019921047

DEDICATED TO

THE PIONEERS WHO SETTLED THE WEST

I arrived at the legendary city of Tombstone in Cochise County, Arizona.

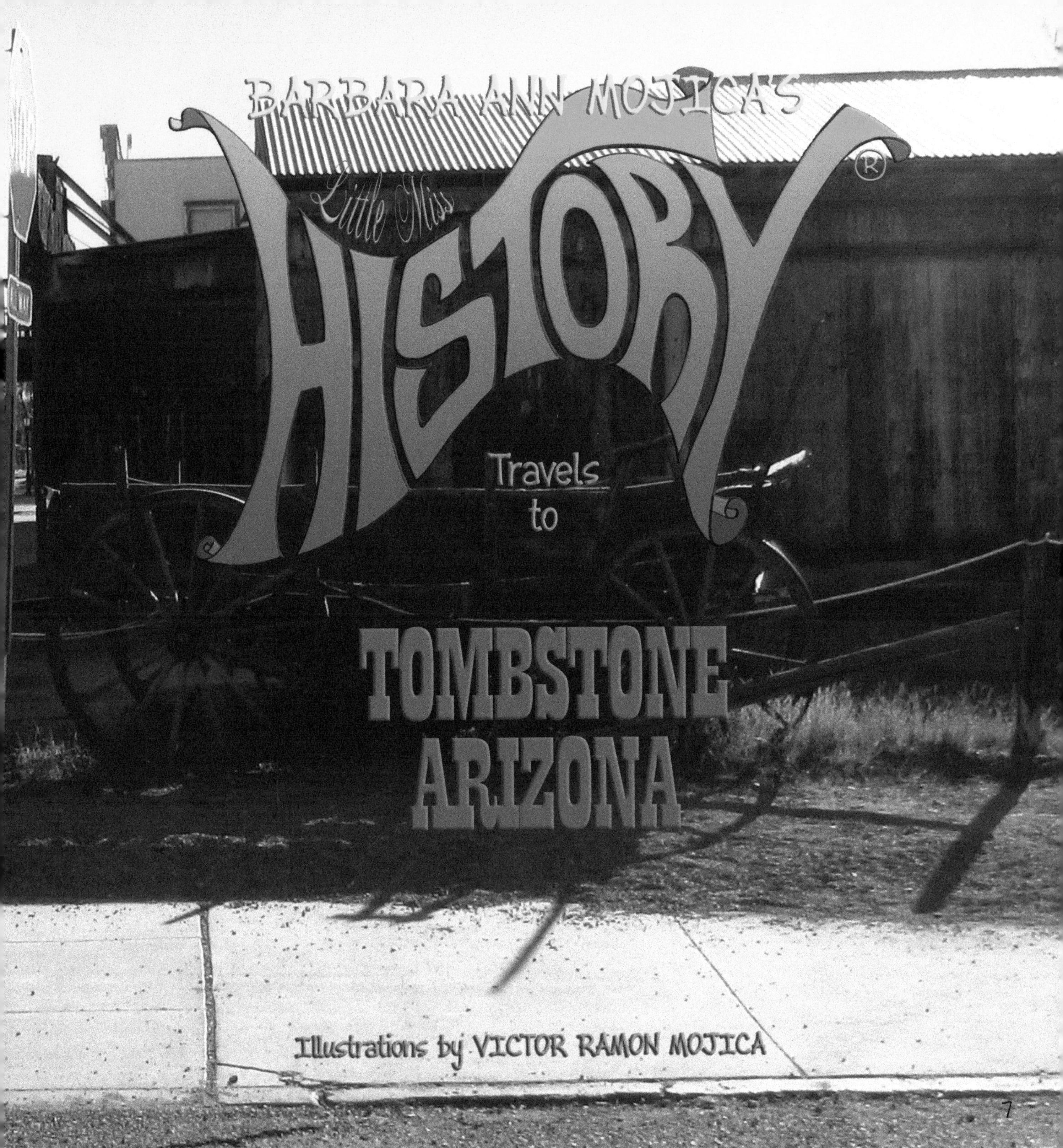

BARBARA ANN MOJICA'S

Little Miss

HISTORY ®

Travels to

TOMBSTONE ARIZONA

Illustrations by VICTOR RAMON MOJICA

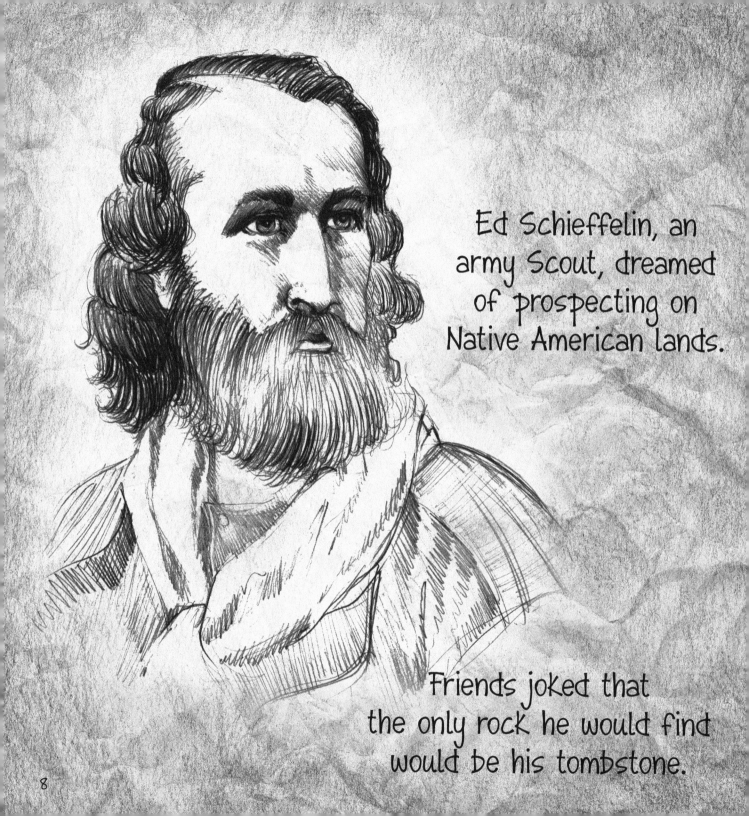

Ed Schieffelin, an army scout, dreamed of prospecting on Native American lands.

Friends joked that the only rock he would find would be his tombstone.

8

When he found a fifty-foot silver vein in 1877, he named his claim "Tombstone," but it soon dried up.

The Lucky Cuss Mine, 1880.

Schieffelin covered the cky Cuss e in 1878.

In 1878, Schieffelin set up a second mine, the "Lucky Cuss Mine". It became one of the richest silver mines in Tombstone.

9

Other mines soon sprang up like the "Tough Nut," "Contention," and the "Good Enough" mine.

The miners moved their tents and shacks to mesas above these mines.

Two years later, Tombstone had a bowling alley, a school, banks, newspapers, an ice house, churches, and an ice cream parlor.

The town size exploded in the 1880s. Silver mines produced forty to eighty-five million in silver bullion.

They decided to name their growing town, "Tombstone."

Its population increased from one hundred to fourteen thousand in a span of seven years.

Entertainment took many forms. Miners could choose from 110 saloons, 14 gambling halls, and dance halls.

The wealthy attended operas at Schieffelin Hall ...

... and shows at The Bird Cage Theater.

John P. Clum founded
The Tombstone Epitaph newspaper
on May 1, 1880 ...

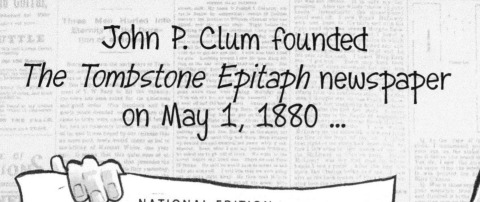

... and it's still
publishing today.

Many Chinese immigrants settled in Tombstone.

China Mary was one of them. Her real name was Sing Choy.

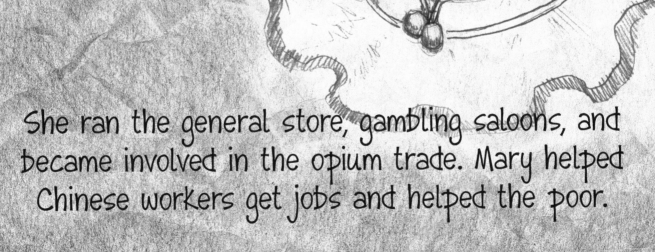

She ran the general store, gambling saloons, and became involved in the opium trade. Mary helped Chinese workers get jobs and helped the poor.

John Haughton Slaughter led a colorful life. Born in Texas, he fought for the Confederates in the Civil War.

Slaughter won election to Sheriff of Cochise County in 1866.

Slaughter arrested outlaws like The Jack Taylor Gang, and assisted the US Calvary in tracking Geronimo, the infamous Apache warrior.

John Swain Slaughter arrived in Tombstone with John Slaughter and his family in 1879. The former slave lived to nearly 100. This monument honors him in Boothill Graveyard.

JOHN SWAIN (SLAUGHTER)
BORN JUNE 1845 FORMER SLAVE WHO CAME TO
TOMBSTONE 1879 DIED FEB. 8, 1945 - ERECTED BY THE
PERSONNEL AT FORT HUACHUCA AND FRIENDS OF
TOMBSTONE IN MEMORY OF A WORTHY PIONEER

Tombstone sits near the Mexican border. That made it popular for stealing cattle.

●TOMBSTONE

The "Cowboys" gang, Ike and Billy Clanton, Frank and Tom McLaury, and Billy Claiborne, added to the area's lawlessness.

Ike Clanton

The Earp brothers, Wyatt, Virgil, and Morgan arrived in Tombstone between 1879 and 1880.

Wyatt Earp

22

They attempted to keep law and order in the town.

23

This led to the gunfight at the OK Corral on October 26, 1881.

24

It actually happened in an empty lot on Fremont Street.

The Earp brothers and Doc Holiday killed Billy Clanton, Frank McLaury, and Tom McLaury.

But the town faced other dangers. By the mid 1880s, the mines penetrated the water table causing floods.

Owners invested in specialized water pumps.
(Picture: Courtesy of the Arizona Historical Society)

In 1881 a lit cigar thrown into a barrel of whiskey started a fire that destroyed 66 buildings.

One year later a fire in a Chinese laundry destroyed 100 buildings.

Another fire in 1866 incinerated the Grand Central hoist and pumping plant. The city seemed destined to become a ghost town.

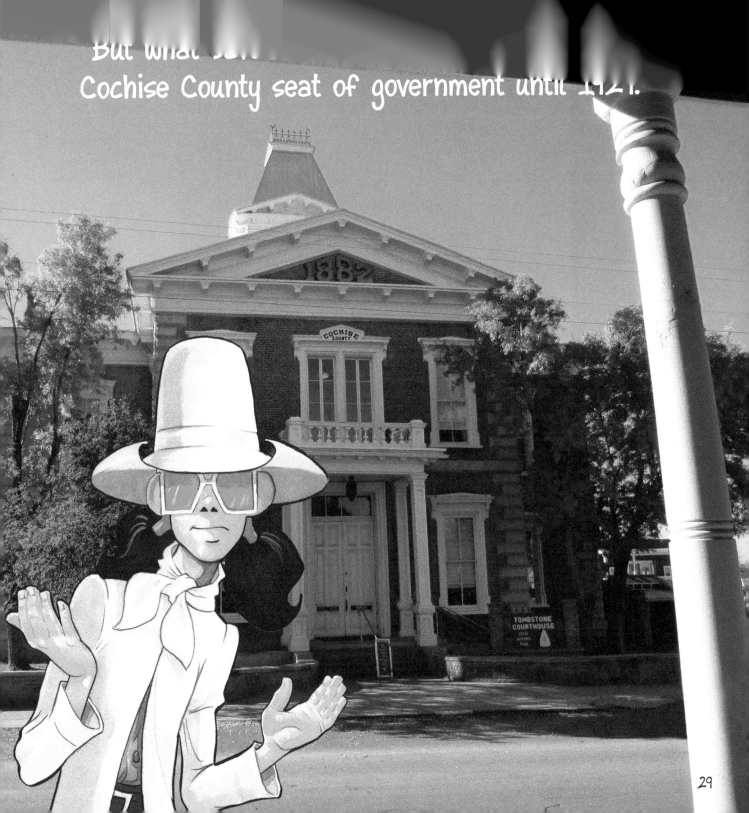

But what [...]
Cochise County seat of government until 1929.

Today, The Courthouse
is a museum.
It contains treasures
from old Tombstone
like these...

REWARD!
$250

$25 REWARD

WYATT EARP'S STRAIGHT RAZOR
MADE IN SHEFFIELD, ENGLAND.

Sheriff Henshaw was presented
this badge by his Deputies.

Next to the courthouse is a reconstruction of the original gallows that burned down in 1912.

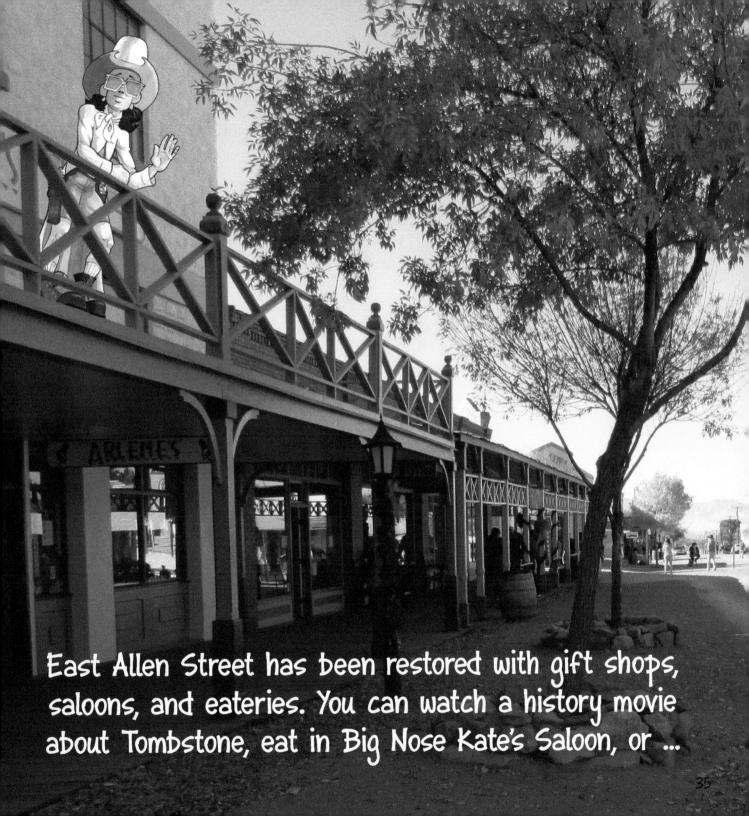

East Allen Street has been restored with gift shops, saloons, and eateries. You can watch a history movie about Tombstone, eat in Big Nose Kate's Saloon, or ...

... watch saloon brawls and shootouts near the OK Corral.

It's a short drive from town to
Boothill Cemetery, originally known as
"The Old Cemetery," founded in 1878.

THE CITY OF TOMBSTONE WELCOMES YOU TO THE LEGENDARY
BOOTHILL GRAVEYARD

BOOTHILL ENTRANCE

The Old Cemetery got its name of "Boothill" because
many buried there died with their boots on.

You can find the graves of Tom McLaury, Frank McLaury and Billy Clanton there.

Sing Choy, better known as
China Mary, is buried there too.

It's getting dark. Time to leave our trip of the Old West and "ride into the Sunset."

GLOSSARY

Boot Hill – a small burial ground in Tombstone, Arizona

Bullion – precious metals in the form of bars or coins

Confederate sympathizer – one who agreed with the Southern states during the Civil War

County seat – the place where government buildings and offices are found

Gambling – to play a game in which you can win or lose money

Gallows – a wooden structure used to hang criminals

Incinerate – to destroy completely by burning

Mesa – a raised piece of flat land with steep sides that drop off

GLOSSARY continued...

Museum – a collection of objects of artistic, cultural, historical, or scientific importance

Opium – a reddish-brown heavy-scented addictive drug prepared from the juice of the opium poppy, used as a narcotic and in medicine to relieve pain

Outlaws – people who are on the run and have broken the law

Prospector – a person who searches for valuable minerals

Reconstructed – rebuild something like the original

Water pump – a machine used to move water or recycle it

Water table – the level under the ground where water can be found

BARBARA ANN MOJICA'S

HISTORY

Travels
to

INDEPENDENCE HALL
& The Museum of the American Revolution

Illustrations by VICTOR RAMON MOJICA

CPSIA information can be obtained
at www.ICGtesting.com
Printed in the USA
BVHW021821060121
596531BV00005B/10

9 780998 915494